CompTIA
Cloud Essentials
Exam: CLO-001

Practice Questions
Version 1

www.ipspecialist.net

Document Control

Proposal Name	:	CompTIA Cloud Essentials Certification Exam Objectives
Document Version	:	1.0
Document Release Date	:	
Reference	:	CompTIA-Cloud-Essentials-Practice-Questions

Feedback:

If you have any comments regarding the quality of this book, or otherwise alter it to better suit your needs, you can contact us through email at info@ipspecialist.net

Please make sure to include the book title and ISBN in your message

About IPSpecialist

IPSPECIALIST LTD. IS COMMITTED TO EXCELLENCE AND DEDICATED TO YOUR SUCCESS.

Our philosophy is to treat our customers like family. We want you to succeed, and we are willing to do anything possible to help you make it happen. We have the proof to back up our claims. We strive to accelerate billions of careers with great courses, accessibility, and affordability. We believe that continuous learning and knowledge evolution are most important things to keep re-skilling and up-skilling the world.

Planning and creating a specific goal is where IPSpecialist helps. We can create a career track that suits your visions as well as develop the competencies you need to become a professional Network Engineer. We can also assist you with the execution and evaluation of proficiency level based on the career track you choose, as they are customized to fit your specific goals.

We help you STAND OUT from the crowd through our detailed IP training content packages.

Course Features:

- ❖ Self-Paced learning
  - Learn at your own pace and in your own time
- ❖ Covers Complete Exam Blueprint
  - Prep-up for the exam with confidence
- ❖ Case Study Based Learning
  - Relate the content with real life scenarios
- ❖ Subscriptions that suits You
  - Get more, pay less with IPS Subscriptions
- ❖ Career Advisory Services
  - Let industry experts plan your career journey
- ❖ Virtual Labs to test your skills
  - With IPS vRacks, you can evaluate your exam preparations
- ❖ Practice Questions
  - Practice Questions to measure your preparation standards
- ❖ On Request Digital Certification
  - On request digital certification from IPSpecialist LTD

About the Authors:

This book has been compiled with the help of multiple professional engineers. These engineers specialize in different fields e.g. Networking, Security, Cloud, Big Data, IoT etc. Each engineer develops content in her/his specialized field that is compiled to form a comprehensive certification guide.

About the Technical Reviewers:

Nouman Ahmed Khan

AWS-Architect, CCDE, CCIEX5 (R&S, SP, Security, DC, Wireless), CISSP, CISA, CISM is a Solution Architect working with a major telecommunication provider in Qatar. He works with enterprises, mega-projects, and service providers to help them select the best-fit technology solutions. He also works as a consultant to understand customer business processes and helps select an appropriate technology strategy to support business goals. He has more than fourteen years of experience working in Pakistan/Middle-East & UK. He holds a Bachelor of Engineering Degree from NED University, Pakistan, and M.Sc. in Computer Networks from the UK.

Abubakar Saeed

Abubakar Saeed has more than twenty-five years of experience, Managing, Consulting, Designing, and implementing large-scale technology projects, extensive experience heading ISP operations, solutions integration, heading Product Development, Presales, and Solution Design. Emphasizing on adhering to project timelines and delivering as per customer expectations, he always leads the project in the right direction with his innovative ideas and excellent management.

Muhammad Yousuf

Muhammad Yousuf is a professional technical content writer. He is Cisco Certified Network Associate in Routing and Switching, holding a Bachelor's Degree in Telecommunication Engineering from Sir Syed University of Engineering and Technology. He has both technical knowledge and industry sounding information, which he uses perfectly in his career.

Uzair Ahmed

Uzair Ahmed is a professional technical content writer holding a Bachelor's degree in

Computer Science from PAF-KIET University. He has sound knowledge and industry experience in SIEM implementation, .NET development, machine learning, Artificial intelligence, Python and other programming and development platforms like React.JS Angular JS Laravel.

Afreen Moin

Afreen Moin is a professional Technical Content Developer. She holds a Degree in Bachelor of Engineering in Telecommunications from Dawood University of Engineering and Technology. She has a great knowledge of computer networking and attends several training programs. She possesses a keen interest in research and design related to computers, which reflects in her career.

Heba Dorazahi

Heba Dorazahi is a Technical Content writer. She has completed her bachelor's degree with a major in Telecommunication Engineering from Sir Syed University of Engineering & Technology. Throughout her academic studies, she gained extensive research and writing skills. She has done online courses of network security and cryptography to develop her expertise.

Free Resources:

With each workbook you buy from Amazon, IPSpecialist offers free resources to our valuable customers.

Once you buy this book you will have to contact us at info@ipspecialist.net or tweet @ipspecialistnet to get this limited time offer without any extra charges.

Free Resources Include:

Exam Practice Questions in Quiz Simulation: IP Specialists' Practice Questions have been developed keeping in mind the certification exam perspective. The collection of these questions from our technology workbooks is prepared to keep the exam blueprint in mind covering not only important but necessary topics as well. It is an ideal document to practice and revise for your certification.

Career Report: This report is a step by step guide for a novice who wants to develop her/his career in the field of computer networks. It answers the following queries:

- Current scenarios and future prospects
- Is this industry moving towards saturation or are new opportunities knocking at the door?
- What will the monetary benefits be?
- Why to get certified?
- How to plan and when will I complete the certifications if I start today?
- Is there any career track that I can follow to accomplish specialization level?

Furthermore, this guide provides a comprehensive career path towards being a specialist in the field of networking and also highlights the tracks needed to obtain certification.

Our Products

Technology Workbooks

IPSpecialist Technology workbooks are the ideal guides to developing the hands-on skills necessary to pass the exam. Our workbook covers official exam blueprint and explains the technology with real life case study based labs. The content covered in each workbook consists of individually focused technology topics presented in an easy-to-follow, goal-oriented, step-by-step approach. Every scenario features detailed breakdowns and thorough verifications to help you completely understand the task and associated technology.

We extensively use mind maps in our workbooks to visually explain the technology. Our workbooks have become a widely used tool to learn and remember the information effectively.

vRacks

Our highly scalable and innovative virtualized lab platforms let you practice the IP Specialist Technology Workbook at your own time and your own place as per your convenience.

Quick Reference Sheets

Our quick reference sheets are a concise bundling of condensed notes of the complete exam blueprint. It's an ideal handy document to help you remember the most important technology concepts related to certification exam.

Practice Questions

IP Specialists' Practice Questions are dedicatedly designed for certification exam perspective. The collection of these questions from our technology workbooks are prepared to keep the exam blueprint in mind covering not only important but necessary topics as well. It is an ideal document to practice and revise your certification.

CompTIA Certifications

CompTIA certification program is a vendor-neutral certification program that recognizes the best certifications in IT world. From the beginning till now CompTIA launched more than two million certifications.

The CompTIA Cloud Essentials certification focuses on the real-world issues and practical solutions of cloud computing in business and IT. It is the preferred cloud certification for business professionals and non-IT staff. Although it is not a challenging technical certification, but it is concept based on the principles of cloud computing.

CompTIA certifications are grouped by skill set. Currently, CompTIA certs fall into four areas: Core, Infrastructure, Cybersecurity and Additional Professional certifications. The certification of CompTIA cloud essentials lies in the Additional Professional area.

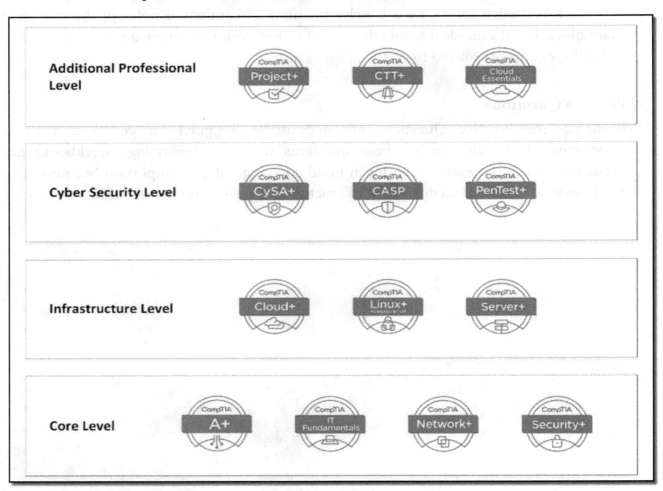

Figure 1- CompTIA Offering Certification Programs

How does CompTIA certifications help?

CompTIA certifications are a de facto standard in networking industry, which helps you boost your career in the following ways:

1. Gets your foot in the door
2. Screen job applicants
3. Validate the technical skills of the candidate
4. Ensure quality, competency, and relevancy
5. Improve organization credibility and customer's loyalty
6. Meet the requirement in maintaining organization partnership level with OEMs
7. Helps in job retention and promotion

CompTIA Certification Tracks

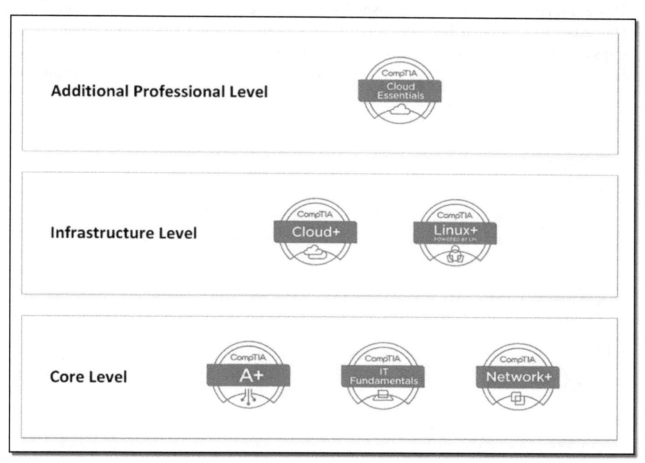

Figure 2- CompTIA Certification Tracks

About the CompTIA Exam

Exam Number:	CLO-001
Associated Certifications:	CompTIA Cloud Essentials
Duration:	60 minutes (60-70 questions)
Available Languages:	English, Japanese, Portuguese, Simplified Chinese and Thai
Registration:	Pearson VUE

This exam tests the candidate's knowledge of cloud services from a business perspective. The expertise validated includes the business value of cloud computing, cloud types, steps to successful adoption of the cloud, impact and changes on IT service management, as well as risks and consequences.

Practice Questions

1. Which of the following option opposes outsourcing to Public Cloud computing only?
   A. There are no upfront CAPEX costs for hardware
   B. Infrastructure is stored within a datacentre
   C. Contracts are in years as opposed to days or months
   D. Internal IT staff moves from one organization to another

2. Which of the following ITIL procedures uses consumer stats for individual cloud service offerings?
   A. Supplier Management
   B. Information Security Management
   C. Service Level Management
   D. Continuous Service Improvement

3. How can an organisation execute a plan for IaaS effectively?
   A. Open up internal databases with web service access
   B. Standardize on a limited set of virtual machines
   C. Continuously execute performance analytics
   D. Take inventory of the application portfolio and select external suppliers

4. Which of the following procedures need to be altered to better manage the cloud's Change Management?
   A. Software Distribution
   B. Hardware Maintenance
   C. Security Management
   D. Financial Chargeback

5. Which of the following is a typical problem in implementing cloud computing for business and IT leaders?
   A. Technical maintenance of current IT assets
   B. Security of current IT solutions
   C. Current cost structure of IT
   D. Quality of web-based user interfaces

6. A company adopts a public computing system based on SaaS cloud to migrate a mission critical application. Which of the following capabilities are the most probable to be lost?
   A. Centralized management of user access to the application
   B. Aversion of the software that will be accessed in the cloud
   C. The ability to access the application from the internal company network
   D. The ability to perform fine grained customizations to the software

7. Which of the following may deteriorate user response times?
   A. Low network bandwidth and high network latency
   B. High network latency and high volume of data sored
   C. High CPU usage and low network bandwidth
   D. Low network bandwidth and high volume of data stored

8. One of the contractual statements made by the cloud provider as part of a critical SaaS implementation is a requirement for scheduled maintenance. This has a direct impact on which of the following?
   A. Service Design
   B. Service Strategy
   C. Service Transition
   D. Service Operation

9. Which of the following cloud computing hazards are linked to compliance?
   A. Cross-charging policies that are handled by both clients
   B. Access rights that are handled by a cloud provider
   C. Capacity management that is handled by a cloud provider
   D. Provider reputation

10. Which of the following cloud service features enhances the company advantages of mobile computing the most?
    A. Security
    B. Hardware Independence
    C. Distribution over the Internet
    D. Time to Market

11. Which of the following is an adverse cloud computing company effect?

A. It lowers the company's overall application processing availability
B. It slows down the company's ability to deal with server capacity issues
C. It is more difficult to ensure policy compliance
D. It is difficult to implement problem management

12. Which of the following BEST defines the cloud computing that allows services to be easily accessible?
A. Scalability
B. Integrity
C. Availability
D. Confidentiality

13. Which of the following is the best way to mitigate cloud computing security and privacy issues?
A. Allowing only cloud administrators to have access to cloud resources
B. Removing firewalls and access control routers from the network
C. Removing virtualized hardware from the organization
D. Implementation and enforcement of a comprehensive security policy

14. Which of the following are the cloud features that accelerate growth, implementation, and general market time?
A. Network Pooling
B. Rapid Elasticity
C. Cloud Bursting
D. Universal Access

15. Which of the following kinds of organisations due to legal requirements would NOT profit from cloud computing?
A. Large Marketing Agencies
B. Online Library
C. Social Media Sites
D. Medical Facility

16. How does cloud computing affect the operation of the service?
A. The provisioning of servers and services is quicker or ceases to be an issue
B. Cloud computing is more cost effective

C. The provisioning of servers and services can be much slower

D. The security level will increase

17. Which of the following is a cloud computing benefit that can boost business value?
    A. Hardware Dependence
    B. Scalability
    C. Fixed Costs
    D. Security

18. Since the execution of a cloud infrastructure, the work description of a senior network administrator has altered from being responsible for keeping the network infrastructure hardware to being more of a leadership role. Which of the following has been impacted the MOST by the change in job responsibility?
    A. Service Transition
    B. Service Design
    C. Service Strategy
    D. Service Operation

19. An organisation intends to host a critical application situated at the ISP's data center on two redundant leased servers. Which of the following is an example of this?
    A. IaaS
    B. Public Cloud
    C. PaaS
    D. SaaS

20. Which of the following is the MOST significant effect on the management of service levels of cloud computing?
    A. Capacity can be more elastic
    B. Scarcity of resources can occur if not monitored
    C. External providers can deny a capacity increase when required
    D. Providers measure their own performance

21. Which of the following is the distinction between outsourcing of cloud computing and IT?

A. IT outsourcing is not based on open standards

B. The service levels of cloud computing are much better

C. Contracts with cloud providers can be changed much quicker

D. Only IT outsourcing works with external staff

22. A company is implementing a substitute system that has application components internally hosted and various application components hosted by separate cloud suppliers as software as a service. Which of the following is the architecture's challenge?

A. Elasticity

B. Complexity

C. Time to Market

D. Cost Saving

23. Which of the following are the prevalent elements of platform as a service and software as a service? (Select two)

A. Both allow the OS to be patched by the customer

B. Both take advantage of the incremental scalability

C. Both require the customer to maintain the hardware

D. Both provide granular access to the backend storage

E. Both implement hardware abstraction

24. How can cloud computing assistance decrease the hazards associated with integrity?

A. Cloud computing makes it easier to have a backup available

B. Cloud computing makes it easier to give people access to data in the cloud

C. Cloud computing makes it easier to have redundancy capabilities

D. Cloud computing makes it easier to monitor access and usage of data

25. A high number of variations of different virtual servers is indicated by which of the following?

A. Lack of manpower to monitor the virtual machines

B. Lack of physical servers to accommodate the different virtual servers

C. Lack of automation of virtual machine image manufacturing

D. Lack of an automated provisioning process of the virtual machines

26. A public cloud subscribes to an organisation. Which of the following is NOT dependent on the vendor by the subscriber?
    A. Internet Bandwidth and Packet Latency
    B. Data Backups
    C. Infrastructure Availability
    D. Service Level Agreement

27. A software development company would like to use their own software to deploy all their application development to the cloud. The cloud type that they are likely to choose to introduce is which of the following?
    A. IaaS
    B. SaaS
    C. XaaS
    D. PaaS

28. A business attempts to understand the impact of adopting cloud computing for the delivery of the latest services on IT service management. Which of the following stages of the lifecycle would probably be evaluated for these effects?
    A. Transition
    B. Design
    C. Operation
    D. Strategy

29. Cloud computing is strongly dependent on which of the following virtualization features? (Select two)
    A. Information Sharing
    B. User Federation
    C. Hardware Independence
    D. Scalable Resource
    E. Simplistic Setup

30. In which of the following scenarios would an organization use a Hybrid Cloud as the BEST choice?
    A. A retail organization that needs to maintain all processing in their own data center
    B. A large development firm that creates applications for the customer to host on

their cloud

    C. A financial organization that must keep all data under their control

    D. A security organization that performs a large percentage of penetration testing

31. Which of the following constraint would be considered in a Private Cloud for the maintenance without downtime?

    A. Organizational direct attached storage

    B. Organizational SAN

    C. Encrypted shared drive

    D. Vendor leased co-hosted storage

32. The capacity to scale resources on demand in cloud computing gives advantages to the company in which of the following respects?

    A. Allowing a third party to manage service delivery ensures lower staffing costs

    B. It is more cost effective to pay for what is needed rather than paying for peak demand upfront

    C. Shorter contracts and less capital expenses reduce expenditures to the IT budget

    D. Fewer in-house servers lower the power consumption of the data center

33. How can economic hazards associated with the cloud be managed?

    A. Credit cards must be used for handling transactions

    B. By renegotiating license agreements

    C. By making sure that cloud assets are generating revenue

    D. By eliminating legacy IT systems

34. A Chief Information Officer would take which of the following routes to implement a cloud solution following a lifecycle approach to IT Service Management?

    A. Decide whether to implement on the cloud; choose XaaS provider; design application; choose where to develop the service application; operate the service application in the cloud

    B. Decide whether to implement the application on the cloud; choose an IaaS provider; choose whether to develop the service in-house; operate the service application in the cloud

    C. Choose the SaaS provider; design the application; choose whether to develop

the service application in-house or outsource; operate the service application in the cloud

    D. Strategize which IaaS provider to use; design the application; transition the development process to the cloud; operate the service application in the cloud

35. When a company intends to introduce a cloud network by pursuing the ITIL standard, which of the following is the FIRST constraint of account?
    A. Current Productivity
    B. Use of Current Skills
    C. Cost of Implementation
    D. Business Needs

36. Cloud services benefit companies seeking to move from capital expenses to operating expenses. True or false?
    A. True
    B. False

37. Which of the following is the best instance of a monthly hosting fee for a cloud vendor that changes according to price allocations?
    A. The company's fee varies based on the number of their IT staff required to support the infrastructure
    B. The company's fee varies based on the number of servers needed to house data in the data center
    C. The company's fee varies based on the projected quarterly revenue of the client's company
    D. The company's fee varies based on the energy consumption of each server in the data centre

38. Which of the following approaches should be evaluated with a direct cost back technique?
    A. CPU Cycles Used
    B. Technical Staff
    C. Power and Cooling Consumed
    D. Square Footage Cost

39. A Chief Information Officer (CIO) of a company wishes to guarantee fast elasticity for the cloud solution of the business. Which of the following cloud types should

he choose?
- A. Private Community Cloud
- B. Private Cloud
- C. Public Cloud
- D. Community Cloud

40. Synchronization of updates is _____ than replicating data across locations because it gives better assurance that data is always _____.
- A. Better, up to date
- B. Better, secure
- C. Worse, up to date
- D. Worse, secure

41. The IT department has moved its email from the business to a cloud provider based on the web. Which of the following dependencies placed on the cloud computing vendor will impact the MOST on all the staff of the company?
- A. Maintainability of Service
- B. Location of Service
- C. Availability of Service
- D. Cost of Service

42. Recently, a company has introduced a federated Hybrid Cloud solution that will enable the rapid and dynamic allocation of resources under high demand, the rapid implementation of its Disaster Recovery Plan (DRP), and the Continuity of Operations (COOP). Given this implementation, the IT director is MOST likely concerned about:
- A. Eliminating security risks
- B. Hiring additional IT staff
- C. Maintaining strategic flexibility
- D. Reducing OPEX allocations

43. A company intends to introduce an internal virtualized infrastructure to provide on-demand storage to its staff that will be available over the public internet via a web interface. This is an example of which of the following?
- A. Private Cloud
- B. Hybrid Cloud

C. Public Cloud

D. Community Cloud

44. A supplier provides storage, processing, memory, and network bandwidth to various tenants, using physical and virtual resources. This is an example of which of the following cloud characteristics?
   A. On-Demand Self-Service
   B. Measured Service
   C. Rapid Elasticity
   D. Resource Pooling

45. From the following, which is an important factor for maintaining strategic flexibility?
   A. Elasticity
   B. Integrity
   C. Return on Investment
   D. Vendor Lock-in

46. A current capability is being moved into the cloud. Capacity management issues have been seen before and an activity is being performed to figure present and future volumes. From the following lifecycle stages, in which of these is it likely to be performed?
   A. Design
   B. Transition
   C. Strategy
   D. Operation

47. From the following, which one is an example of cloud-related security risk?
   A. Losing network connectivity
   B. Not knowing what the cloud provider will charge
   C. Not having enough software licenses
   D. Storing customer data at a service provider

48. Traditional Licensing models do not fit well with scalable resources, cloud computing is therefore used to bring new challenges to _____ management.

A. Commercial

B. Service

C. Financial

D. Legal

49. Which of the following cloud computing model is MOST typically accessed through web services?

A. SaaS

B. PaaS

C. IaaS

D. None of the above

50. By using cloud computing services, which of the characteristics will allow a company to market its product to the public?

A. Client-server application modules

B. Web-based application modules

C. Desktop virtualization throughout the company

D. Client-based training modules

51. Which of the following risk will be a result of cloud computing providers limiting their Service Level Agreement (SLA) liabilities?

A. Legal Risk

B. Security Risk

C. Compliance Risk

D. Privacy Risk

52. From the following, which are the appropriate steps to migrate a backwards compatible application into the Cloud?

A. Decommission the internal infrastructure, purchase services from the cloud provider, and enable them for business users

B. Purchase services from cloud provider, migrate the user accounts, and disable the internal infrastructure

C. Migrate the data and rebuild the application using APIs

D. Assess, proof of concept, migrate data, migrate application, automation/scaling and optimizing

53. By what method can an organization effectively execute a SaaS strategy?
    A. Manage the risks associated with bringing in external providers
    B. Open up internal databases with web service access for easier access
    C. Continuously execute performance analytics to monitor providers
    D. Standardize on a limited set of virtual machines to increase security

54. An organization chooses to reduce its IT work force by employing an external organization to achieve various aspects of IT administration, such as software patch management, desktop virtualization, and remote network maintenance. The organization will still have technicians for maintenance and storage administration. Which of the following services has this organization availed?
    A. PaaS
    B. Virtualization
    C. Outsourcing
    D. IaaS

55. A cloud computing vendor is aiming on distributing applications to consumers. The objective is to simplify the deployment of database functionality while removing the need for consumers to manage the Operating System and application patching. Which of the following types of solution is the vendor proposing?
    A. Software-as-a-Service
    B. Anything-as-a-Service
    C. Infrastructure-as-a-Service
    D. IT-as-a-Service
    E. Platform-as-a-Service

56. What is the difference between cloud computing and virtualization when IaaS is implemented?
    A. Cloud computing may use virtualization, while virtualization does not require cloud services
    B. Both a cloud and a virtual solution will provide additional programmers for application development
    C. Boxed, retail versions of office suite software must be used for consistent licencing
    D. All hardware is maintained on-site by current IT staff and managers

57. A company is substituting its core insurance platform with internally hosted systems and applications hosted in the cloud. Which of the following actions is a part of service transition?
  A. Ensure that monitoring controls are implemented by the cloud provider to ensure that the system is highly available and that performance can be measured
  B. Ensure that as part of the change management process the events are sequenced to handle the cloud provider and that they have resources available
  C. Ensure that the capacity and storage is available to meet the current and future demands of the solution of the cloud provider's infrastructure
  D. Ensure that the SLA's for availability have been well documented and agreed to as part of the contract arrangement between the two companies

58. For logging into SaaS solutions, digital identities can be issued by everyone except:
  A. A user
  B. The current organization
  C. The SaaS provider
  D. A third-party identity provider

59. From the following components, which component is relevant of the cloud ecosystem?
  A. Hypervisors
  B. Security Procedures
  C. Trained IT Staff
  D. Image Factory

60. Why should a developer consider the cloud ecosystem when developing applications?
  A. The role of the IT department will change
  B. The development process needs to change
  C. This can speed up the development process
  D. Cloud providers will do application development

61. An authorised hold has been demanded on an employee's mailbox by the organization's legal office. The organization IT group is incapable of implementing the authorised hold since the email system has recently been commissioned to the cloud. Which of the following has the organization failed to consider when moving

the email service to the cloud?

A. Archival Procedures
B. Business Continuity Plan
C. Retention Policy
D. Email Restoration Process

62. When mitigating risks in a cloud environment while avoiding effect on performance, which of the following is true?

A. When securing cloud resources, it is always a best practice to encrypt all data stored in the cloud
B. When securing cloud resources, only the most sensitive data should be secured
C. When securing cloud resources, data security is not an issue
D. When securing cloud resources, it is always a best practice to use the strongest security on the most sensitive data

63. Due to implementation of cloud computing, which of these IT processes are likely to become more important?

A. Request Fulfilment Management
B. Troubleshooting Management
C. Project Management
D. Capacity Management

64. From the following, which is included in a compliance audit?

A. Analysing identity management and access controls
B. Analysing cloud provider Service Level Agreements (SLAs)
C. Analysing the provider release calendar
D. Analysing chargeback agreements

65. What is the most significant difference between SaaS and IaaS?

A. SaaS is used only for Public Clouds
B. IaaS can be secured and encrypted
C. SaaS is accessible anywhere
D. IaaS can test network configurations

66. What is the MOST important skill needed by cloud vendor to communicate with the subscriber?

A. Industry Best practices

B. Visualization

C. Customer service

D. Project management

67. Which important new skill should be developed by an IT organization in the context of cloud computing?
    A. Incident Management
    B. Technology Upgrade Monitoring
    C. Security and Risk Management
    D. Provisioning Services

68. What is the function of an orchestration service from the following?
    A. Assemble functional requirements for application development
    B. Configure application clusters with web services
    C. Enable and disable load balancers
    D. Manage the starting and stopping of application server clusters

69. What are the benefits of cloud computing solution for an application development provider? (Select two)
    A. Reduced storage requirements
    B. Reduced bandwidth usage
    C. Reduced development timeframe
    D. Reduced complexity for users
    E. Reduced training time for new developers
    F. Reduced cost

70. From the following options, what can be deployed by a cloud provider to reduce storage costs?
    A. Journaling file systems
    B. Two-factor authentication
    C. Data de-duplication
    D. Data encryption

71. An organization contracted a third party vendor to give email and spam/anti-malware filtering services. Given the scenario, the type of cloud service provided by

the vendor is BEST described as?

A. SaaS
B. CaaS
C. PaaS
D. IaaS

72. Cloud computing is valued according to _____ or has _____, rather than having upfront charges.

A. A recurring subscription, usage-based charges
B. Number of users, a yearly contract
C. A yearly contract, usage-based charges
D. Recurring subscription, a yearly contract

73. For what reasons are traditional chargeback systems not compatible with cloud computing?

A. Cloud computing can be more expensive than in-house capacity
B. Resources that are used can fluctuate throughout the budget cycle
C. Cloud computing is low cost and does not accommodate charge back fees
D. Licensing models can become outdated quickly

74. "https" is considered more secure than "http" when accessing cloud services. True or false?

A. True
B. False

75. One of the vital reasons for buying technology services from various providers is to:

A. Keep vendor prices down
B. Avoid vendor lock-in
C. Encourage vendor control
D. Influence governmental organizations

76. When using an external cloud service provider, what is the MOST significant risk a business can face in terms of continuity?

A. Virtual server failure
B. Vendor going out of business
C. Vendor being purchased

D. Unauthorized access to customer data

77. Which of the cloud characteristics BEST describe the following scenario: As part of a cloud provider's services, customers can arrange another virtual machine when required without human interaction with the provider?
    A. Rapid Elasticity
    B. Broad Network Access
    C. On-Demand Self-Service
    D. Measured Service

78. What are the essential steps to take when creating a virtual server?
    A. Select a machine image to run, select an application set to run, select security credentials
    B. Select a machine image to run, select an application set to run, select the size of the virtual machine
    C. Select an application set to run, select security credentials, select the size of the virtual machine
    D. Select a machine image to run, select security credentials, select the size of the virtual machine

79. Eucalyptus is an open-source software framework that provides a platform for private cloud computing implementation on computer clusters. This is an example of:
    A. On-demand software
    B. PaaS
    C. IaaS
    D. SaaS
    E. None of the above

80. Why do business users prefer to interact with cloud providers directly, instead of doing it through IT department?
    A. It reduces financial risks to the business
    B. The IT department does not accommodate variable costs
    C. They can better measure the provider's quality
    D. They can use their own payment options

81. What is the MOST important business continuity risk?
    A. Incomplete Service Level Agreements (SLAs)
    B. Network connectivity interruption
    C. Privacy laws
    D. Providers going out of business

82. From the following options, which one refers to the strategic exit?
    A. Re-host in-house
    B. Change the cloud provider
    C. Change the system applications
    D. All of the above

83. Which aspect of public cloud computing should a company consider to ensure information security?
    A. Data Integrity
    B. Network Hardware
    C. Firewall Specifications
    D. Server Type

84. Cloud usage metering plan takes into account which of the following customer chargeback choices?
    A. Cost Amortization
    B. Shared Cost
    C. Cost Allocation
    D. Direct Cost

85. From the following, what can influence the payment of monthly service fee paid by Company A for Company B to host their cloud, such that Company A's fee increases as their company grows?
    A. Connectivity Speed
    B. Uptime Requirements
    C. Amount of Data Stored
    D. Confidentiality of the Data

86. Which applications are MOST suitable for a cloud computing pilot?
    A. Applications that are currently expensive to maintain because of

    interconnections

    B. Applications with high risk and little business value

    C. Applications that are easy to migrate and have some business value

    D. Legacy applications that are coupled to specific hardware and systems software

87. What is BEST used when setting up security for services used within a Public Cloud?

    A. SNMP

    B. LDAP

    C. SSL

    D. SFTP

88. From the following business benefits, what does cloud computing and IT outsourcing have in common?

    A. Flexible contracts

    B. Reduction of capital expenditures

    C. Clarity and budgeting ease of upfront costs

    D. Improvement of employee skills sets

89. An organization is using third party provided, internet-based cloud service. When providing cloud resources, what can the third party NOT guarantee?

    A. Capacity

    B. Network Path

    C. Cost

    D. Scalability

90. What does IT outsourcing and cloud computing have in common?

    A. Pay as you go agreements

    B. Short-term financial commitment

    C. Tailor-made applications based on client needs

    D. Vendor lock-in potential

91. An organization has decided to apply a third-party hosted service so they have numerous virtual machines if needed. From the following, what service does this signify?

    A. VTP

B. Private Cloud

C. VPN

D. Public Cloud

92. For what reason can cloud computing be a challenge in connection to compliance risk (for example compliance with the Sarbanes-Oxley Act)?
   A. Industry regulations change more frequently to ensure compliance
   B. It is harder to limit the provider's liability in the contract
   C. It makes it harder to know where a company's physical assets are
   D. It makes it harder to know where a company's important assets are

93. From the following, what must a vendor fulfil to provide successful IaaS solutions? (Select two)
   A. Physical Security
   B. Network Maintenance
   C. Application Development
   D. Web-based Application Maintenance
   E. Application Configuration Settings

94. Tracing data centers near a target market is the outcome of which strategic initiatives?
   A. Geoproximity
   B. Geodiversity
   C. Geography
   D. Localization

95. After moving the organization's whole data center infrastructure to a private IaaS arrangement, while in the meantime keeping up the present system and server logical design, the IT director made half of the IT building staff redundant. The rest of the staff has now moved their focus from an everyday server maintenance and upkeep job to more of a service provisioning, performance, and reporting job. Which of the following was MOST affected by this transfer?
   A. Service Strategy
   B. Service Transition
   C. Service Design

D. Service Operation

96. From the following, which confidentiality risk is introduced by cloud computing?
    A. Having files stored on the servers of a cloud provider
    B. Government regulations require data to be disclosed
    C. Digitizing information makes it easier to copy
    D. Company information can be transmitted electronically

97. How can cloud computing BEST reduce costs for a business?
    A. Utilizing services as needed
    B. Utilizing local resources
    C. Increasing available data storage
    D. Increasing sales potential

98. What is the benefit of Public Cloud computing?
    A. Reduces OPEX costs for application and databases
    B. Adds flexibility and agility to enterprise architecture
    C. Contributes to the quality of user input data
    D. Enhances fixed expenditures for hardware and software

99. From the following, which asset have risks linked to a cloud provider going bankrupt?
    A. Data stored at the provider
    B. Investment in servers at the provider
    C. Machine capacity at the provider
    D. Cloud management tools housed at the provider

100. A software development platform is currently being moved from an in-house system to a cloud-based PaaS. Which of the following development aspect is MOST likely to be appropriate in the PaaS condition?
    A. Cloud environments only support agile development. The software development team will need to change from their waterfall SDLC methodology before migrating
    B. No expected change in software development process when migrating from in-house to PaaS
    C. PaaS providers do not allow customers with their own software development

teams to write new applications on the cloud platform

    D. Familiarization will be required with cloud provider-based APIs, web services and development frameworks

101. What is one key difference between cloud computing and IT outsourcing?

    A. Typically, industry definitions state that cloud computing and IT outsourcing are synonymous terms with the same meaning

    B. Cloud computing provides only external IT equipment to a company, whereas outsourcing involves external only resources managing internal company equipment

    C. Cloud computing generally allows on-demand utilization, whereas outsourcing is typically defined by contract terms

    D. Cloud computing only works when there is satisfactory internet connectivity whereas, outsourcing requires dedicated WAN links

102. Which one of the following is a reason for which the military facility cannot fully embrace cloud computing?

    A. High degree of confidentiality and operational assurance

    B. Constantly changing data and accessibility needs

    C. Constantly changing and unpredictable workloads

    D. The associates cost and infrastructure needs

103. What kind of risk does an organization face if the cloud provider stops serving?

    A. Legal Risk

    B. Continuity Risk

    C. Financial Risk

    D. Confidentiality Risk

104. What role does an IT department play when selecting cloud computing providers?

    A. Help understand performance parameters

    B. Help understand and explain the application lifestyle

    C. Help understand provider quality

    D. All of the above

105. An organization might want to move an application to the cloud, which resides

on a single server in their data center. The server has two drives, one of which has the operating framework, and the other hosts the application data. The operating system has been indicating about the errors as of late and the application data was corrupted last Friday at 4:00PM. Data is backed up each day at 1:00AM. What is the BEST choice for moving this application to the cloud?

    A. Clone or P2V the server with the application drive to the cloud platform and copy the Operating System to the cloud server

    B. Setup a server in the cloud, install an Operating System, install and configure the application, and copy the data to the cloud server from last Thursday's backup

    C. Clone or P2V the server with both drives to the cloud platform

    D. Setup a server in the cloud, install an Operating System, install the application and copy the data to the cloud server from last Friday's backup

106. What characteristics does a Private Cloud have?

    A. Services are managed by a third-party provider

    B. Infrastructure is managed by an independent service provider

    C. Services are accessed by members outside of the organization

    D. Services are restricted to members of the same organization

107. What does cloud computing and outsourcing have in common from the following options?

    A. Shift from CAPEX to OPEX

    B. Reduced compliance cost

    C. Simplified security management

    D. Reduced system architecture complexity

108. _____ have rights to reveal whatsoever information they want about _____ and limit further usage of that information by anyone.

    A. Individuals, others

    B. Individuals, themselves

    C. Companies, themselves

    D. Companies, others

109. Which service will enable a company to integrate internal identity management services with a cloud provider in order to provide single sign-on over the internal

and cloud-hosted environments?

    A. Virtualization

    B. Outsourcing

    C. Role-based Authentication

    D. Federation

110. From the following, what is one example of SaaS?

    A. Hosted network hardware

    B. Hosted database software and development tools

    C. Offshore help desk support

    D. Hosted email software

111. From the following, what is the influence of cloud computing on application development?

    A. SaaS delays the time to market for most applications

    B. SaaS inhibits vender interoperability on applications platform

    C. SaaS allows for a shorter time to market for some applications

    D. SaaS allows for open-source application development

112. Which of the following would be a successful cloud service strategy implementation?

    A. An organization has identified services investments partners and delivery channels designed to meet requirements

    B. An organization has managed the investment portfolio for services available to users of the cloud services

    C. An organization has identified patterns of business activities that use services and manage activities to influence demand

    D. An organization has managed budgeting and accounting for cloud services needed   for   the   organization

113. Which of the following would be a risk, if an IT department is only a provider of infrastructure?

    A. Business users will bypass the IT department

    B. Cloud providers will take over the role of the IT department

    C. Service providers will bypass the IT department

D. All of the above

114. Twitter is a service that enables users to exchange short text messages. This is an example of:

    A. SaaS

    B. PaaS

    C. IaaS

    D. QoS

115. Which of the following service factors must be efficiently managed in a Cloud computing environment by a SaaS provider?

    A. Availability

    B. User Acceptance

    C. Application Access Levels

    D. Client Background Checks

116. The IT department of a company spends numerous hours a day maintaining database server's hardware. The company migrates the server to the cloud. Which of the following IT department's job responsibility has been MOST impacted by this change?

    A. Service Strategy

    B. Service Design

    C. Service Transition

    D. Service Operation

117. Which of the following early cloud computing examples was used in the form of web-based applications for software engineering purposes and required interoperability between different systems?

    A. Virtual Private Networks (VPNs)

    B. Distributed Computing

    C. Desktop Virtualization

    D. Service-Oriented Architecture (SOA)

118. Which of the following is a reason to be interested in cloud computing for business

users?

A. Desire for improved security

B. Desire for vendor lock-in reduction

C. Desire for improved user experience

D. Desire for reducing compliance issues

119. In order to guarantee that different organizations can authenticate and share fundamental user accounting data, which of the following must be enforced by a cloud provider?

A. Virtualization

B. Federation

C. Self Service

D. Scalability

120. Why does request fulfilment in a cloud environment become more complex?

A. Processes must be redesigned with the user experience in mind

B. The IT service team must be expanded

C. All processes must become automated

D. Users should be aware of the benefits before changes to the process are incorporated

121. In which of the following ways do IT outsourcing and cloud computing differ?

A. Cloud computing is much cheaper

B. Hardware and software assets are typically customizable

C. Cloud computing services are typically much more scalable

D. IT outsourcing promotes innovation

122. For businesses, elastic computing is essential as it relates to which of the following cloud features?

A. Scalability

B. Integrity

C. Distribution

D. Security

123. Which of the following describes what is meant by the component of the ITIL Service Strategy?

   A. Designing the solution to the ITIL specifications

   B. Defining processes required to manage the solution

   C. Understanding the intended customer and what services are required

   D. Ensuring changes are designed to meet customer expectations

124. How can the internal IT department respond to cloud computing effectively?

   A. By outsourcing all IT services

   B. By becoming an external cloud provider

   C. By solely focusing on security issues

   D. By becoming an internal cloud provider

125. To BEST roll out desktop images from a cloud network, which of the following should be applied?

   A. Virtual Servers

   B. Federation

   C. Backup and Recovery

   D. Automation and Self Service

126. Which application types are appropriate for a cloud computing pilot?

   A. Marginal Applications

   B. Desktop Productivity Applications

   C. Mission-Critical Applications

   D. Legacy Applications

127. An organisation needs its internal systems and its externally hosted SaaS financing scheme to be federated so that a user does not have to re-authenticate. This is an example of which of the following?

   A. Biometric Scanning

   B. Open Authentication

   C. Single Sign-on

   D. Multifactor Authentication

128. A university has moved several services to a third-party cloud provider from its inner infrastructure. Which of the following is MOST important to the university to guarantee a suitable security posture?

    A. Regular patching applied by the university

    B. Governance and oversight by the cloud provider

    C. Antivirus checks performed by the cloud provider

    D. SLA and metrics requested by the cloud provider

129. Which of the following would help the IT department of an organization set their goals and expectations for a cloud computing solution?

    A. Service Design

    B. Service Strategy

    C. Service Transition

    D. Service Operation

130. Which of the following cloud services would rent hardware, computing, network space, and internet storage?

    A. PaaS

    B. XaaS

    C. SaaS

    D. IaaS

131. A particular cloud deployment has been developed specifically for financial services companies to consume. Which of the following BEST defines this sort of cloud environment?

    A. Private Cloud

    B. Community Cloud

    C. Public Cloud

    D. Hybrid Cloud

132. Which of the following cloud computing services requires the MOST participation of the in-house staff of a company?

    A. SaaS

    B. PaaS

C. MaaS

D. Iaas

133. A financial firm has selected an external cloud service provider to provide some capabilities that were used to be done in-house. Which of the following would provide the BEST amount of coverage by continuous assertion to the financial business so that the service provider achieves an appropriate security posture?

A. Perform a risk assessment annually and mandate that any unacceptably high risks are mitigated

B. Define required security service levels, agree on security evaluation criteria and perform regular compliance checks based on the service level and evaluation criteria

C. Ensure that the service provider aligns to an industry standard such as ISO 27000 series or another regulatory compliance framework and request that they self-monitor annually

D. Perform a penetration test every 6 to 12 months and mandate that any unacceptable high issues or risks are mitigated

Answers

1. **A.** (There are no upfront CAPEX costs for hardware)
   Explanation: Public cloud computing suppliers use standardized, shared infrastructure, often using comparatively inexpensive hardware product that is why there are no upfront CAPEX costs for hardware.

2. **C.** (Service Level Management)
   Explanation: ITIL describes Service Management as a collection of specific organizational capacities in the form of services to provide value to clients. ITIL Service Level Management aims to negotiate customer service level agreements and design services in line with accepted service level objectives.

3. **B.** (Standardize on a limited set of virtual machines)
   Explanation: Infrastructure-as-a-Service (IaaS) is a form of cloud computing that provides virtualized computing resources over the internet. In order to implement IaaS strategy, an organization can normalise the use of virtual machines.

4. **A.** (Software Distribution)
   Explanation: Change Management (CM) is one of the ITIL procedures that control the life cycle of IT Infrastructure. Distribution of software is the method that needs to be altered to better handle change management in the cloud.

5. **B.** (Security of current IT solutions)
   Explanation: When speaking about cloud computing, security is always an element to consider. Service providers promise to be safer than physical data centers. Cloud applications must safeguard the transmission of information over the network.

6. **D.** (The ability to perform fine grained customizations to the software)
   Explanation: The capacity to fine-grained software customization is probable to be lost if a business adopts a public SaaS cloud based computing scheme to migrate a mission-critical application.

7. **B.** (High network latency and high volume of data stored)
   Explanation: High network latency and high volume of data generate blockages

within the network, thereby decreasing the quantity of information that can be transmitted over a period of time and can lead to deteriorating response times.

8. **D.** (Service Operation)

   Explanation: SaaS Service Operation relates to a technique of providing hosted software applications to customers in a cloud computing environment.

9. **B.** (Access rights that are handled by a cloud provider)

   Explanation: Cloud computing risk associated with compliance is the access right handled by cloud providers.

10. **C.** (Distribution over the Internet)

    Explanation: Mobile devices allow people to access data and information from anywhere at any time and internet distribution is the business advantage of mobile computing.

11. **C.** (It is more difficult to ensure policy compliance)

    Explanation: Cloud technology is intrinsically distributed and as a result, compliance is a shared responsibility between organisations and service providers. In cloud computing it is difficult to ensure policy compliance, which has negative impact on business

12. **C.** (Availability)

    Explanation: Availability represents the concept of access to services, tools and information, anywhere and anytime. Availability best defines the correct cloud computing capabilities that allow services to be easily accessible.

13. **D.** (Implementation and enforcement of a comprehensive security policy)

    Explanation: If the cloud service providers have a written security plan of policies, then the security of the data will be guaranteed. If the cloud service provider do not have a security policy written plan, then the cloud is not safe and security of the data cannot be guaranteed as they do not have a written plan of security policies.

14. **B.** (Rapid Elasticity)

    Explanation: Rapid Elasticity is a cloud computing term for scalable provisioning,

or the ability to provide scalable services. Rapid elasticity accelerates growth, implementation, and general market time.

15. **D.** (Medical Facility)

   Explanation: Legally protected data, such as health information or personal identifiers, should never be stored in the cloud unless they are encrypted during storage.

16. **A.** (The provisioning of servers and services is quicker or ceases to be an issue)

   Explanation: Server and service provisioning is faster or ceases to be a problem when cloud computing affects service operations.

17. **B.** (Scalability)

   Explanation: Cloud hosting offers many benefits to businesses. It is cost-effective, extremely reliable and provides scalability, flexibility, agility, high performance and security.

18. **B.** (Service Design)

   Explanation: Service design has been affected the most by the change in job responsibility after the implementation of a cloud infrastructure, a senior level network administrator's job description has changed from being responsible for maintaining the hardware of the network infrastructure to more of a management position, ensuring that the cloud vendor provides the services specified in the contract with the company.

19. **C.** (IaaS)

   Explanation: Infrastructure-as-a-Service (IaaS) is an internet based immediate computing infrastructure that is supplied and managed. IaaS enables you to prevent the cost and difficulty of purchasing and handling your own physical servers and other infrastructure of your data center. Each resource is provided as a distinct service element, and for as long as you need, you only need to rent one.

20. **A.** (Capacity can be more elastic)

   Explanation: With a cloud environment, a single service level management process can exist, but Service Level Packages should be defined, monitored, and managed for each service. Capacity elasticity is the greatest effect of cloud

computing on service level management.

21. **C.** (Contracts with cloud providers can be changed much quicker)

    Explanation: The user has control over its processor with outsourcing, through the contract and its guidelines to the processor. However, it is frequently thought that cloud users lose control with cloud computing. The main difference between cloud computing and IT outsourcing is that cloud supplier contracts can be altered much faster.

22. **B.** (Complexity)

    Explanation: A company that implements a system substitute has internally hosted application components and various application components hosted by various cloud suppliers as software.

23. **B & D.** (Both take advantage of the incremental scalability) & (Both provide granular access to the backend storage)

    Explanation: Platform-as-a-Service (PaaS) is a cloud computing model that provides hardware and software tools by a third-party provider. Software-as-a-Service (SaaS) is a software distribution model, where a third-party provider hosts applications and makes them accessible over the internet to customers. Both take advantage of the incremental scalability and provide the backend storage with granular access.

24. **A.** (Cloud computing makes it easier to have a backup available)

    Explanation: Data integrity ensures that data is of high quality, accurate and unmodified. Cloud computing supports efficient backups of information. In case of data loss, data corruption, and data integrity problems, information backups assist to ensure data recovery.

25. **C.** (Lack of automation of virtual machine image manufacturing)

    Explanation: Various virtual servers indicate the lack of automation of virtual machine image manufacturing.

26. **A.** (Internet Bandwidth and Packet Latency)

    Explanation: Bandwidth and latency both describe the speed and capacity of a network. When an organization subscribes to a Public Cloud, internet bandwidth

and packet latency will not depend on the vendor.

27. **D.** (PaaS)

   Explanation: PaaS makes the development, testing, and deployment of applications quick, simple, and cost-effective. PaaS is the sort of cloud that a software development company needs in order to organize all of its applications.

28. **D.** (Strategy)

   Explanation: Strategy is the lifecycle stage where a company tries to comprehend the impacts of cloud computing for the delivery of latest IT services.

29. **C & D.** (Hardware Independence) & (Scalable Resources)

   Explanation: Virtualization turns physical hardware into virtual machines, while cloud computing is a type of service that is used to store the transformed data. Cloud computing is strongly dependent on virtualization features such as hardware independence and scalable resources.

30. **B.** (A large development firm that creates applications for the customer to host on their cloud)

   Explanation: Hybrid Cloud is a cloud computing environment that utilizes a mixture of on-premises, Private Cloud and third-party, orchestration public cloud services between two platforms. Hybrid Cloud is the best choice for a large development company that makes applications for the client to host on their cloud.

31. **B.** (Organizational SAN)

   Explanation: Storage Area Network (SAN) enables system maintenance to be performed without causing downtime, and can also significantly improve disaster recovery time. In a Private Cloud, Organizational SAN would be considered.

32. **B.** (It is more cost effective to pay for what is needed rather than paying for peak demand upfront)

   Explanation: Cloud computing can benefit your company with lower expenses, flexible capacity, enhanced agility and much more.

33. **C.** (Making sure that cloud assets are generating revenue)

Explanation: For Cloud users, a big hazard is underestimating the original price of building the system and it can be managed by ensuring that Cloud assets generate income.

34. **D.** (Strategize which IaaS provider to use; design the application; transition the development process to the cloud; operate the service application in the cloud)

Explanation: A Chief Information Officer would gather the right information, make better decisions based on evidence and deliver more value together in an IT Service Management lifecycle approach.

35. **D.** (Business Needs)

Explanation: ITIL standards provide a strong basis for organizations adopting cloud computing and cloud based services. If a business needs to introduce a cloud network by pursuing the ITIL standard, business demands are the first consideration element.

36. **A.** (True)

Explanation: "CAPEX vs. OPEX" refers to the requirement of capital expenditure of maintaining your own data center, while using an external cloud service that provides pay-as-you-go service, which falls into ongoing operating expenditures.

37. **B.** (The company's fee varies based on the number of servers needed to house data in the data centre)

Explanation: The fee for the company varies depending on the amount of servers required to house information in the data center.

38. **B.** (Technical Staff)

Explanation: IT chargeback is an accounting approach that relates IT services, equipment or software expenses to the company unit where they are being used providing technical staff to be evaluated with a technique of direct cost chargeback.

39. **C.** (Public Cloud)

Explanation: Elasticity basically implies that your platform can handle sudden, unanticipated, and unusual loads. A Chief Information Officer (CIO) of a company who wishes to ensure fast elasticity for the cloud solution of the business would

likely choose Public Cloud.

40. **A.** (Better, up to date)

Explanation: Synchronizing updates are better than replicating information locally as it provides better certainty that information is always up to date.

41. **C.** (Availability of Service)

Explanation: Availability refers to the uptime of a system, a network of systems, hardware and software that collectively provide a service during its usage. Availability of service will have the most effect on all the employees as the IT department has moved the company's email to a web-based cloud provider.

42. **A.** (Eliminating security risks)

Explanation: Business Continuity Plans usually concentrate on continuing business services in the case of any kind of interruptions, whether based on IT or otherwise. Disaster Recover Plans often refer to the strategy of a company if something happens to vital business data, and how to restore/ recover that data.

43. **B.** (Hybrid Cloud)

Explanation: The Hybrid Cloud is a cloud environment made up of a combination of on-premises Private Cloud resources combined with third-party Public Cloud resources to provide a company's employees with on demand storage. This will be available over the public internet via a web interface.

44. **D.** (Resource Pooling)

Explanation: The computing resources of the provider are pooled to serve various consumers using a multi-tenant model, with distinct physical and virtual resources dynamically assigned and reassigned according to consumer demand.

45. **D.** (Vendor Lock-in)

Explanation: Vendor lock-in refers to a situation, where a customer is dependent on a vendor for products or services and cannot easily transition to a competitor's product or service.

46. **A.** (Design)

Explanation: Migration of a capability can take up a lot of space and since there

have been issues in past regarding data storage, changes are to be made in the design stage of the lifecycle to increase enough storage so that the future volumes do not face such issues.

47. **D.** (Storing customer data at a service provider)

    Explanation: Files in the cloud are most likely to be hacked without security measures in place. Storing data with the provider is a major risk as there are chances of data being stolen even if the file is encrypted.

48. **C.** (Financial)

    Explanation: Traditional Licensing Models do not fit well with scalable resources. Cloud computing solves that problem but brings about new challenges in financial management like security, privacy, availability, etc.

49. **B.** (PaaS)

    Explanation: Platform-as-a-Service (PaaS) provides Cloud components to certain software while being used mainly for applications.

50. **B.** (Web-based application modules)

    Explanation: Web-based application is any program that is accessed over internet. This will help a company market its product to a larger customer base.

51. **A.** (Legal Risk)

    Explanation: Service Level Agreements (SLAs) is a commitment between a service provider and a client. SLAs guarantee clients a certain level of service and uptime. In case if the service and uptime is limited, there is a chance of a legal risk being faced by the provider.

52. **D.** (Assess, proof of concept, migrate data, migrate application, automation/scaling and optimizing)

    Explanation: Backward Compatible program refers to new applications that support the features of older version. Moving these applications to cloud greatly improves security. The migration of these apps differ from the forward compatible apps being made.

53. **A.** (Manage the risks associated with bringing in external providers)

Explanation: Software-as-a-Service (SaaS) uses internet to deliver applications, which are managed by third party vendor to its users. An organization can successfully implement SaaS strategy, if it can manage the risks linked with bringing third party vendors.

54. **C.** (Outsourcing)

Explanation: Outsourcing involves contracting an outside source to manage various functions of a company. An organization can decide to outsource its IT functions in order to gain world class capabilities and to reduce costs.

55. **A.** (Software-as-a-Service)

Explanation: Software-as-a-Service (SaaS), uses internet to deliver applications, which are managed by third party vendor, to its users. SaaS makes it easier for the customer to access sources provided by the cloud service provider without downloading any application.

56. **A.** (Cloud computing may use virtualization, while virtualization does not require cloud services)

Explanation: Infrastructure-as-a-Service (IaaS), is an instant computing infrastructure, provisioned and managed over the internet. When implementing IaaS in an organization, cloud services might require visualisation but visualisation can work without cloud services.

57. **B.** (Ensure that as part of the change management process the events are sequenced to handle the cloud provider and that they have resources available)

Explanation: When transitioning from core platform to cloud services, a business should always make sure that a cloud provider with proper resources is contacted.

58. **A.** (A user)

Explanation: Digital identity is online identity adopted by an individual, organization, or electronic device. When logging into SaaS solutions, digital identity can be issued by an organization, SaaS provider, or a third party identity provider but not a user.

59. **D.** (Image Factory)

Explanation: Cloud ecosystem is a complex system of interdependent

components that work together to enable cloud services. An image factory builds image for a variety of Operating Systems and cloud ecosystems.

60. **C.** (This can speed up the development process)

    Explanation: Cloud ecosystem is a complex system of interdependent components that work together to enable cloud services. Cloud ecosystem helps in making applications because it is easier to aggregate data and analyze how each part of the system affects the other part.

61. **C.** (Retention Policy)

    Explanation: Retention policy refers to an organization's policy of retaining data for operational use. Since the email system has already been outsourced, taking a legal hold of the mailbox can proof to be a hard job.

62. **B.** (When securing cloud resources, only the most sensitive data should be secured)

    Explanation: When mitigating risks, a company should make sure to secure all the sensitive data. Data privacy is one of the main problems faced when moving data in cloud computing and should be done to avoid sensitive data from being stolen.

63. **D.** (Capacity Management)

    Explanation: When adopting cloud computing, the biggest issue faced by the businesses is of capacity management. Capacity management has to be done right in order to prevent workload in the future, making capacity management one of the most important process when working with cloud computing.

64. **A.** (Analysing identity management and access controls)

    Explanation: Compliance audit in simple terms, is an audit undertaken to check if the company is following the terms of an agreement. Analysing identity management and access control are the most important things present in the compliance audit. Identity management is assigning and maintaining an individual's identity, while access control is verifying the identity of an individual at the point of access.

65. **D.** (IaaS can test network configurations)

    Explanation: Software-as-a-Service (SaaS), uses internet to deliver applications,

which are managed by third party vendors, to its users. Infrastructure-as-a-Service (IaaS) is an instant computing infrastructure, provisioned and managed over the internet. The most significant difference between the two is that IaaS can test network configurations.

66. **C.** (Customer Service)

Explanation: Customer Service is an important skill a cloud provider should possess when communicating with the customer. Good customer service not only helps in maintaining good relationship with the customer but can also help business continuity due to loyal customers.

67. **D.** (Provisioning Services)

Explanation: With the growth of cloud computing, IT organizations need to develop more skills to stay in market. One of the skill needed is of provisioning cloud services. Provisioning services or cloud provisioning refers to the processes of deploying and integrating cloud computing services within an IT enterprise.

68. **D.** (Manage the starting and stopping of application server clusters)

Explanation: In cloud computing, orchestration services refer to arranging and coordinating automated tasks required for cloud automation. One of the functions, which an orchestration service performs is to manage the starting and stopping of application clusters. Application clustering refers to turning multiple servers into one cluster so that it acts like a single system.

69. **C. & F.** (Reduced development timeframe) & (Reduced cost)

Explanation: An application development provider is a company that provides access to applications or related services to individuals and enterprises over the internet. Cloud computing services benefit an application development provider by reducing the cost and timeframe needed for development.

70. **C.** (Data de-duplication)

Explanation: Data de-duplication is a technique used to remove duplicate data. This technique can be used by cloud service providers to remove duplicate data to reduce storage costs.

71. **A.** (SaaS)

Explanation: Software-as-a-Service (SaaS), uses internet to deliver applications, which are managed by third party vendor, to its users. The third party vendor providing the services basically works on SaaS model.

72. **A.** (A recurring subscription, usage-based charges)

Explanation: Unlike traditional systems, cloud computing is priced on the basis of usage or have subscriptions based pricing rather than upfront costs.

73. **B.** (Resources that are used can fluctuate throughout the budget cycle)

Explanation: Traditional chargeback systems are not compatible with cloud computing due to varying costs, which can cause the budget cycle to fluctuate as the resources that are used fluctuate according to the usage.

74. **A.** (True)

Explanation: "https" stands for 'Hyper Text Transport Protocol Secure' while http stands for 'Hyper Text Transport Protocol' making https more secure to access the website.

75. **B.** (Avoid vendor lock-in)

Explanation: Vendor lock-in refers to a situation where a customer is dependent on a vendor for products or services and cannot easily transition to a competitor's product or service. By distributing vendors, businesses can avoid the vendor lock-in situation.

76. **D.** (Unauthorized access to customer data)

Explanation: Unauthorized access to customer data by external cloud service provider can risk business continuity as customers will no longer trust the business with their personal data. Data breach of any kind can cause business failure.

77. **C.** (On-Demand Self-Service)

Explanation: This service can help user make their own virtual machine whenever needed. It will make the creation of virtual machine a lot faster since no human interaction is involved.

78. **D.** (Select a machine image to run, select security credentials, select the size of the

virtual machine)

Explanation: Virtual server is a server at another location, which multiple website owners can access and use as a server with complete control of it.

79. **E.** (None of the above)

Explanation: Eucalyptus stands for Elastic Utility Computing Architecture for Linking Your Programs to Useful Systems. Eucalyptus give users the ability to run and control entire virtual machines instances across a variety of physical resources. Eucalyptus does not work on any of the famous cloud computing models.

80. **B.** (The IT department does not accommodate variable costs)

Explanation: Businesses usually deal with cloud service providers directly as the IT department does not accommodate variable costs. Variable costs refer to costs that varies with the output.

81. **D.** (Providers going out of business)

Explanation: Businesses are susceptible to disasters varying in size. Business plan is made to help the business owner recover their assets in case of failure. The biggest risk to the continuity of business is of the provider going out of business. This can cause catastrophic damage to the business in case of no contingency plan.

82. **A.** (Re-host in-house)

Explanation: Exit strategy is a contingency plan executed by an entrepreneur to exit their position in an asset at a certain point in time. Re-host in-house is a popular migration strategy to move applications, software and data to cloud with little effort making re-host in-house one of the most popular exit strategy.

83. **A.** (Data Integrity)

Explanation: Data integrity is the maintenance and assurance of the accuracy of the data. Data integrity is the most vital part that a business should consider when ensuring the safety of data on Public Cloud.

84. **C.** (Cost Allocation)

Explanation: Most of the provider's charge is based on the usage of cloud

services. Cost allocation is one of the huge benefit of metering the cloud usage, by doing this, a customer can prevent "runaway" bills.

85. **C.** (Amount of Data Stored)

Explanation: As the organization grows there is a need for more data storage space. More data requires more storage space, which will in turn increase the fee Organization A pays for Organization B to host their cloud.

86. **C.** (Applications that are easy to migrate and have some business value)

Explanation: Moving critical applications to the cloud can cause a business failure if the applications fail. Therefore, the most suitable applications for cloud are the ones which are easy to migrate and the ones that have some business value.

87. **C.** (SSL)

Explanation: Secure Socket Layer (SSL), is a security technology used for establishing a secure link between two systems. For services on Public Cloud, SSL certificate is the best option to prevent criminals from reading and modifying any data.

88. **B.** (Reduction of capital expenditures)

Explanation: IT Outsourcing involves contracting an outside source to manage various functions of a company. Cloud computing is the delivery of computing services over the internet to offer flexible resources.

89. **C.** (Cost)

Explanation: A third party service provider cannot guarantee the costs that a business will incur when using internet-based cloud service. As the costs depends on the usage of the service, hence more data leads to greater costs.

90. **D.** (Vendor lock-in potential)

Explanation: Vendor lock-in refers to a situation where a customer is dependent on a vendor for products or services and cannot easily transition to a competitor's product or service. Both outsourcing and cloud computing have vendor lock-in as a problem.

91. **B.** (Private Cloud)

Explanation: Private Cloud is a type of cloud computing where scalability and self-service is provided through a proprietary architecture but only to a single organization unlike Public Cloud, which offers these resources to multiple organizations.

92. **D.** (It makes it harder to know where a company's important assets are)

Explanation: Compliance risk is the potential for losses and legal penalties if the business fails to meet the terms set by the industry. Cloud computing possess a challenge to compliance risks as it makes it harder for a company to know where their important assets lie.

93. **A& B.** (Physical Security) & (Network Maintenance)

Explanation: Infrastructure-as-a-Service (IaaS) is an instant computing infrastructure, provisioned and managed over the internet. When implementing IaaS in an organization, a vendor should be able to provide physical security as well as network maintenance for the cloud service to keep the data secure and up to date.

94. **A.** (Geoproximity)

Explanation: It depends on what kind of service is being provided by the business. In case of gaming and financial services, it is beneficial to have data centers close by. However for webhosting, a delay of 1 to 2 minutes does not cause an issue, making Geoproximity one of the most important strategic initiative.

95. **B.** (Service Transition)

Explanation: Service transition ensures that the transition of new or modified service is done in an organised way. By reducing the task force and moving organization's entire data center to a cloud, the impact of this transition is mostly on the service transition.

96. **A.** (Having files stored on the servers of a cloud provider)

Explanation: With the introduction of cloud computing came many risks; the biggest risk being privacy. One of the reasons why companies do not upload sensitive data on cloud is the risk of files being stored on the cloud service provider's server.

97. **A.** (Utilizing services as needed)

    Explanation: By using cloud computing, a company can save cost by utilizing services when needed as the cloud service provider will only charge for the services used.

98. **A.** (Reduces OPEX costs for application and databases)

    Explanation: OPEX stands for Operational Expenses. The main benefit of using Public Cloud is the reduction in OPEX costs for applications and databases. OPEX uses pay-as-you-go model, which costs less compared to CAPEX where the long term benefits are considered rather than short term ones.

99. **A.** (Data stored at the provider)

    Explanation: With cloud computing, privacy can be a big issue. For a business hiring cloud services from a provider, the biggest risk will be data stored in the server of the provider. In case of the provider going out of business, this does not only cause privacy issues but can also cause continuity issues for businesses as well.

100. **D.** (Familiarization will be required with cloud provider-based APIs, web services and development frameworks)

    Explanation: Platform-as-a-Service (PaaS) provides cloud components to certain software while being used mainly for applications. When transitioning from an in-house framework to PaaS, a company should familiarize itself with the cloud provider and the APIs, development frameworks and web services a cloud provider can provide. This is likely to make the transition smooth and easy for the organization.

101. **C.** (Cloud computing generally allows for on-demand utilization, whereas outsourcing is typically defined by contract terms)

    Explanation: Cloud computing and outsourcing are both similar in many ways but the key difference between the both is the usage. With cloud computing, the utilization of the services can be done as per the need, whereas in outsourcing, the utilization is defined in the contract.

102. **A.** (High degree of confidentiality and operational assurance)

Explanation: In cloud computing, privacy is a huge risk. Military organizations having high degree of confidentiality and operational assurance cannot fully embrace cloud computing due to a huge risk of data exploitations.

103. **B.** (Continuity Risk)

Explanation: A business with all its applications, data and software on cloud can face a huge continuity risk if the cloud service provider stops the service. This can cause the business to go bankrupt.

104. **D.** (All of the above)

Explanation: An IT department can help select which cloud computing provider is better suited for the business by assessing the quality of the provider and the performance parameters. The department can also help in understanding the application lifecycle.

105. **D.** (Setup a server in the cloud, install an operating system, install the application and copy the data to the cloud server from last Friday's backup)

Explanation: The organization should first setup a cloud server and install an Operating System, similar to the one in the organization's physical server. After performing the initial steps, the organization should refer to the backup done on Friday at 4:00 PM and install the application with the backed up data. The organization should refrain from copying the backup data done at 1:00 AM everyday as it is likely to be corrupted and can stop the further development and usage of the application.

106. **D.** (Services are restricted to members of the same organization)

Explanation: Private Cloud is a type of cloud computing where scalability and self-service is provided through a proprietary architecture but to a single organization, therefore restricting the cloud services to the members of organization only.

107. **A.** (Shift from CAPEX to OPEX)

Explanation: CAPEX stands for Capital Expenses while OPEX stands for Operational Expenses. Both outsourcing and cloud computing have switched from CAPEX to OPEX to reduce costs incurred.

108. **B.** (Individuals, themselves)

Explanation: Every individual has the right to disclose information about themselves. Being the owner of the information disclosed, individuals also have the right to restrict any other party from accessing the disclosed information. The information in no way should be exploited or made use of as serious issues can ensue if the owner decides to take action.

109. **D.** (Federation)

Explanation: To make single-on option available for both internal system and cloud, the company needs to have approval from the federation. A federation refers to a group, which is interested in protecting the rights and the interests of company employees. An approval from federation ensures that the privacy rights of all the employees are preserved.

110. **D.** (Hosted email software)

Explanation: Software-as-a-Service (SaaS), uses internet to deliver applications, which are managed by third party vendor to its users. Hosted email software is one example of SaaS model. An example of hosted email software can be Gmail.

111. **B.** (SaaS inhibits vender interoperability on applications platform)

Explanation: With the rise of cloud computing for application development, most of the organizations are transitioning to cloud computing. In cloud computing, interoperability refers to the ability of customers able to use the same services with various cloud providers. SaaS restrains vendor interoperability in application development.

112. **A.** (An organization has identified services, investments, partners, and delivery channels designed to meet requirements)

Explanation: Cloud computing strategy service will give you a strategic plan for transforming your data center from a traditional computing model into a private cloud service provider. To meet requirements of a successful cloud service, an organization needs to have identified services, investments, partners, and delivery channels designed.

113. **A.** (Business users will bypass the IT department)

Explanation: IT departments are accountable for ensuring that the technology of

an organization works properly and access to business applications and services are maintained. However, there is a risk that business consumers will bypass IT department when it is restricted to the infrastructure provider alone.

114. **A.** (SaaS)

Explanation: SaaS is a software distribution model that also allows users to exchange short text messages on twitter.

115. **A.** (Availability)

Explanation: Since SaaS applications are provided over the internet, users can avail them from any Internet-enabled device and location. Hence, availability must be managed effectively by a SaaS provider in a cloud computing environment.

116. **D.** (Service Operation)

Explanation: Service Operation of the IT department has been impacted the most when its company migrates the server to the cloud during maintenance of the hardware.

117. **D.** (Service Oriented Architecture (SOA))

Explanation: The Service Oriented Architecture is an architectural design that involves service collection in a network that communicates with each other. Service-Oriented Architecture is an example of cloud computing, which is used for software engineering purposes.

118. **C.** (Desire for improved user experience)

Explanation: By moving business to cloud computing, business users can improve efficiency, increase productivity, and save costs also it can enhance user experience.

119. **B.** (Federation)

Explanation: A cloud provider must establish a federation to guarantee that different organizations are able to authenticate and share basic user accounting information.

120. **A.** (Processes must be redesigned with the user experience in mind)

    Explanation: Cloud computing is far more cost-effective and scalable as compared to IT outsourcing.

121. **C.** (Cloud computing services are typically much more scalable)

    Explanation: Cloud computing is far more cost-effective and scalable as compared to IT outsourcing.

122. **B.** (Integrity)

    Explanation: Elastic computing is a cloud computing idea, in which the cloud service provider can easily scale up and down computing resources. Elastic computing can relate to integrity.

123. **B.** (Defining processes required to manage the solution)

    Explanation: ITIL Service Strategy's goal is to decide on a strategy to serve customer. The Service Strategy lifecycle phase determines, which services the IT organisation is to deliver and what capacities need to be developed. The ultimate objective of the organisation is to make the IT work strategically.

124. **B.** (By becoming an internal cloud provider)

    Explanation: By becoming a Private Cloud provider, an internal IT department reacts effectively to cloud computing.

125. **D.** (Automation and Self Service)

    Explanation: Self-service cloud computing needs comprehensive planning to run smoothly and with service mainly being on-demand, automation is essential on the provider's end. Automation and self-service can be implemented to roll out desktop images.

126. **B.** (Desktop Productivity Applications)

    Explanation: Desktop productivity applications are the kinds of apps that are appropriate for cloud computing pilot.

127. **C.** (Single Sign-on)

    Explanation: Single sign-on is a federated identity management that allows an

end user's account information to be used by third-party services so a user does not have to re-authenticate.

128. **B.** (Governance and oversight by the cloud provider)

Explanation: Governance and oversight by the cloud provider is essential to migrate multiple services from their inner infrastructure to a third-party cloud provider in order to guarantee security for the university.

129. **B.** (Service Strategy)

Explanation: Service strategy enables to design, develop and implement service management. It also helps the IT department in an organization to set their objectives and expectations for a cloud computing solution.

130. **D.** (IaaS)

Explanation: IaaS cloud service provides fundamental infrastructure for computing: Servers, Storage, and Networking resources. It is used to rent hardware, computing and networking space, as well as storage over the Internet.

131. **B.** (Community Cloud)

Explanation: A Community Cloud provides a cloud computing solution to a restricted amount of people or organizations that are frequently controlled, managed and protected commonly by all the participating organizations and it is established specifically for financial service companies to consume.

132. **C.** (MaaS)

Explanation: MaaS is an outsourced service that primarily offers security to platforms running on the Internet for business purposes. It is a cloud computing service that has the most involvement from a company's in- house staff.

133. **B.** (Define required security service levels, agree on security evaluation criteria, and perform regular compliance checks based on the service level and evaluation criteria)

Explanation: A financial firm has selected an internal cloud service provider to provide some capacities that were used to be done in-house. Some of the providers that provide the best amount of coverage to the financial company are

the ones that define the necessary level of safety services, agree on safety assessment criteria and conduct periodic compliance inspections based on service levels and assessment criteria.

About Our Products

Other Network & Security related products from IPSpecialist LTD are:

- CCNA Routing & Switching Technology Workbook
- CCNA Security v2 Technology Workbook
- CCNA Service Provider Technology Workbook
- CCDA Technology Workbook
- CCDP Technology Workbook
- CCNP Route Technology Workbook
- CCNP Switch Technology Workbook
- CCNP Troubleshoot Technology Workbook
- CCNP Security SENSS Technology Workbook
- CCNP Security SIMOS Technology Workbook
- CCNP Security SITCS Technology Workbook
- CCNP Security SISAS Technology Workbook
- CompTIA Network+ Technology Workbook
- CompTIA Security+ v2 Technology Workbook
- Certified Information System Security Professional (CISSP) Technology Workbook
- CCNA CyberOps SECFND Technology Workbook
- Certified Block Chain Expert Technology Workbook
- Certified Cloud Security Professional (CCSP) Technology Workbook

Upcoming products are:

- CompTIA Pentest+ Technology Workbook
- CompTIA A+ Core 1 (220-1001) Technology Workbook
- CompTIA A+ Core 2 (220-1002) Technology Workbook
- CompTIA Cyber Security Analyst CySA+ Technology Workbook
- CompTIA Cloud+ Technology Workbook
- CompTIA Server+ Technology Workbook

Note from the Author:

Reviews are gold to authors! If you have enjoyed this book and it helped you along your certification, would you consider rating and reviewing it?

Link to Product Page: